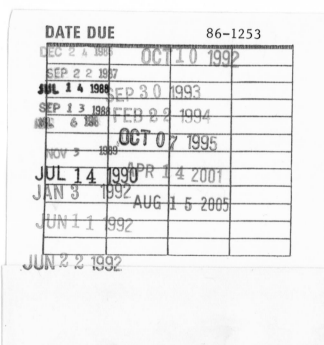

A New True Book

SEASONS

By Illa Podendorf

*This "true book" was prepared
under the direction of
Illa Podendorf,
formerly with the Laboratory School,
University of Chicago*

CP CHILDRENS PRESS, CHICAGO

Oak leaves

PHOTO CREDITS

Candee & Associates—4 (bottom right), 34, 35
(3 photos), 36 (top right), 40 (2 photos)

Tony Freeman—4 (top right), 18 (2 photos), 20
(2 photos)

James P. Rowan—Cover, 10, 12 (top), 17
(right), 19

Jerry Hennen—14, 22 (below)

Lynn M. Stone—2, 4 (top left, bottom left), 12
(bottom), 15 (2 photos), 17 (left), 24 (right), 25,
26 (2 photos), 29 (left), 33, 39, 44 (2 photos)

Margaret Thoma—30 (below), 36 (top left), 43

Alaska Division of Tourism—11

United States Department of Agriculture—16,
29 (right), 30 (above)

Texas State Department of Highways & Public
Transportation —22 (top), 24 (left)

Federal Aviation Administration: FAA—36
(bottom)

Cover-Winter in the city

Library of Congress Cataloging in Publication Data

Podendorf, Illa.
  Seasons.

  (A New true book)
  Previously published as: The true book of seasons.
1955.
  Summary: Explains the changing of seasons and de-
scribes how plants and animals adapt to and prepare for
these changes.
  1. Seasons—Juvenile literature. [1. Seasons]
I. Title.
QH81.P67   1981   574.5'43   81-7751
ISBN 0-516-01647-4   AACR2

86-1253

TABLE OF CONTENTS

The Sun and the Seasons. . . 5

Spring. . . 13

Summer. . . 19

Fall. . . 25

Winter. . . 33

Words You Should Know. . . 46

Index. . . 48

Spring forest

Fall in Wisconsin

Watermelon, a summer treat

Winter

THE SUN AND
THE SEASONS

There are four seasons in a year. They are:

Spring

Summer

Fall

Winter

There are seasons because the earth goes around the sun. And because the earth is tipped.

It takes the earth a year
to go once around the sun.
It is summer when the
part of the earth where we
live is tipped toward the
sun.
It is winter when the
part of the earth where we
live is tipped away from
the sun.

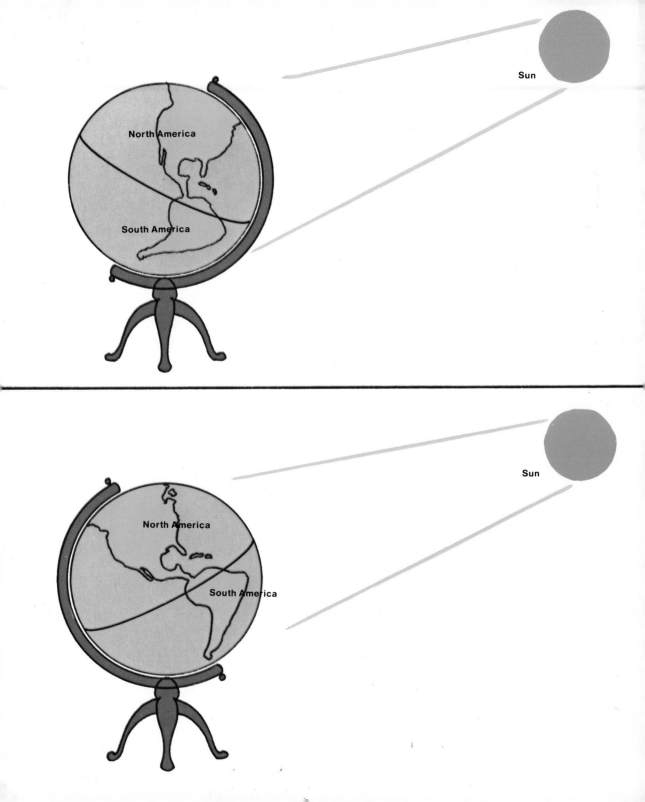

In the winter the sunshine is on more of a slant.

In the summer our shadows are short at noontime.

In the winter our shadows are long at noontime.

Coconut
palms in
the Pacific

In some parts of the
world it is warm almost all
year.

Boys and girls who
live there never see snow.

Eskimo woman and sled dogs in Alaska

In other parts of the
world it is cold almost all
year.

Boys and girls who live
there see a lot of snow.

False Rue Anemone

Skunk Cabbage

SPRING

Many people live in a part of the world where the weather changes with the seasons.

They are glad to see spring come. Snow melts. The grass turns green. The days become warmer.

In the spring it gets light earlier in the morning. It stays light later in the evening.

Robins and many other birds return from the south where they have been all winter.

Birds build nests and eggs hatch in the spring.

Robin eggs
in nest

Cecropia Moth

Toad trilling

Moths and butterflies begin to fly about.

Toads come out of their burrows after a long winter sleep. They hunt for food.

Buds on the trees swell.
Soon they break into
leaves and flowers.

Can you think of other
signs of spring?

Farmers plow their fields.
They make them ready for
planting crops.

Planter

Left: Daffodils and jonquils

Above: Apple orchard in bloom

People work in their gardens. As soon as the ground is ready, they plant seeds.

There are spring showers and warm sunshine. Flowers begin to bloom.

Children bring out their roller skates, jump ropes, baseballs, and bikes.

March, April, and May are spring months.

Common Indian Paintbrush

SUMMER

Many people like summer almost as well as spring. The weather is warm.

Sometimes it is hot. People like to go to the beach when it is hot.

In summer the days are longer than at any other time of the year. They are longer because there are more hours of daylight. The longest day comes in June.

Families go camping in the summer. The summer months are June, July, and August.

Mares with foals

Doe with her fawn

Mother and father birds are busy. They hunt food for their babies.

When summer is over baby birds can care for themselves.

Almost everywhere animals are busy caring for their young.

Some kinds of animals have more than one family in a summer.

Warm rain and bright sunshine make the plants grow.

Farmers harvest their wheat crops. They cut their hay in the summer.

Soon there are many ripe vegetables in the gardens.

Wheat harvesting

Vegetables

Peppers 15

White birch tree and fall leaves

FALL

Fall comes. The days become shorter. Leaves change colors. Some turn yellow and others turn red or brown.

Eastern gray squirrel

Common Milkweed pod and seeds

Families rake the fallen leaves.

Many kinds of seeds are scattered in the fall.

Many animals do things in fall that are helpful to them in winter.

Squirrels gather nuts and hide them.

Toads eat a great deal before they go down into the ground for the winter.

Bears and raccoons eat
a great deal and grow fat.
They hide in dens and
sleep most of the winter.

Geese fly over, going
south. Many kinds of birds
go south in the fall.

Beavers store food. They
make their homes safe
before the ponds freeze
over. The cold weather will
not harm them.

Farmers gather in the corn from their fields. Do you see something else they gather? They gather potatoes, too.

Corn

Potato harvest

Apple tree

Fall harvest

Many trees are full of ripe fruit in the fall. The fruit must be picked carefully.

People store fruits and vegetables for winter. They cook and put part of the food in cans so it will not spoil.

Some fruits and vegetables are prepared and put in a freezer.

They will not spoil if they are properly frozen.

Fall months are September, October, and November. During these months, farmers store food for their animals to eat in the winter.

Frozen stream in Illinois

WINTER

It is very cold in winter.
Sometimes roads are icy.
People must wear warm
clothing.

Horses grow heavier coats in winter.

Horses and some other animals grow heavier coats in winter. They seem to like the cold weather.

There is much snow in the winter. Children like to play in it. They build a snowman and sometimes they build a fort.

Children like to play in snow.

Strong winds pile the snow into high drifts. People shovel the walks.

Snowplows push the snow off streets and highways.

Bears and some other animals sleep in their dens most of the winter.

They almost never go out for food. They ate a great deal in the fall.

Bulbs and roots of plants rest in the ground under the snow.

The snow helps to keep them from freezing. Seeds rest in the ground under the snow, too.

Snow has a lot of air in it. It is the air that helps keep the bulbs, roots, and seeds from freezing.

Children coast on the snowy hills and skate on the frozen ponds.

They do these things during the winter. The winter months are December, January, and February.

The shortest day of the year is in the winter. It comes in December.

It is dark when the children eat their supper. It is dark when they get up in the morning.

Toward spring the days become a little longer.

The snow begins to melt and the moisture goes down into the ground.

Hepatica in melting spring snow

Bird nest in pussy willows

The sunshine is on less of a slant. The days become warmer.

When people see the first robin, they know spring will come soon.

It is fun to live where there are four seasons in a year. Each season is very special for certain reasons.

WORDS YOU SHOULD KNOW

bulb—a round plant part that grows under the ground

burrow(BUR•oh)—a tunnel dug in the ground by an animal

coast (KOHST)—to move down a hill on a sled

coat (KOHT)—fur or hair of an animal

den —the home of a wild animal

drift —to pile up

freeze—to change from a liquid to a solid

harvest (HAR•vest)—to gather in a crop

melt—to change from a solid to a liquid

moisture(mOYs•cher)—water

plow—a farm tool used to break up the soil

raccoon (reh•KOON)—an animal with black markings on his face and a bushy tail

root —the part of a plant that grows down into the ground

season(SEE•zun)—a part of the year

slant—to be tipped; slope

spoil(SPOYL)—to rot so as to be bad to use

store—to put away

toad(TODE)—an animal with rough skin that is much like a frog

weather(WEH•thir)—how hot, cold, sunny, rainy, windy it is at a certain time

INDEX

animals, 23, 27, 28, 32, 34, 37
beach, 19
bears, 28, 37
beavers, 28
birds, 14, 23, 28, 45
bulbs, 38
butterflies, 15
camping, 21
canned food, 31, 32
children, 18, 34, 41, 42
clothing, warm, 33
cold weather, year-round, 11
corn, 29
crops, 16, 24
day, longest, 21
day, shortest, 42
earth, goes around sun, 5, 6
earth, tipped, 5, 6
fall, 5, 25-32, 37
farmers, 16, 24, 29, 32
flowers, 16, 17
frozen food, 31, 32
fruit, 31
gardens, 17, 24
geese, 28
grass, 13
hay, 24
horses, 34
leaves, 16, 25, 27
light, in spring, 14
longest day, 21

months, fall, 32
months, spring, 18
months, summer, 21
months, winter, 41
moths, 15
plowing, 16
potatoes, 29
raccoons, 28
rain, 17, 24
robins, 14, 15
roots, 38
seasons, list of, 5
seeds, 17, 27, 38
shadows, 9
shortest day, 42
showers, 17
snow, 10, 11, 13, 34, 37, 38, 42
snowplows, 37
spring, 5, 13-18, 45
squirrels, 27
summer, 5, 6, 9, 19-24
sun, 5, 6
sunshine, 9, 17, 24, 45
toads, 15, 27
trees, 16, 31
vegetables, 24, 31
warm weather, year-round, 10
wheat, 24
winter, 5, 6, 9, 27, 28, 31, 32, 33-45
year, 6

About the Author

Born and raised in western Iowa, Illa has had experience teaching science at both elementary and high school levels. For many years she served as head of Science Dept., Laboratory School, University of Chicago and is currently consultant on the series of True Books and author of many of them. A pioneer in creative teaching, she has been especially successful in working with the gifted child.